Assessing Your Career Options

A Workbook for
Taking Charge of Change

by Donald L. Double

Assessing Your Career Options
A Workbook for Taking Charge of Change

©1998 by the American Medical Association

Printed in the USA.
All rights reserved.

Additional copies of this book (Product Number 0P206397) may be ordered by calling toll free 800 621-8335.

Internet address: http://www.ama-assn.org

ISBN 0-89970-887-0

BP37:97-325:3M:5/98

About the Author

Donald Double has spent the last two decades assessing and coaching senior executives. He has worked in the medical field for Baxter Travenol, creating and delivering management development programs. He was with the Rehabilitation Institute in Chicago in Human Resources. A consultant for the past sixteen years, he has worked extensively for health care organizations, including the American Medical Association, the American Hospital Association, and the University of Illinois Hospital and Clinics, helping them with executive assessment, coaching, and team building, and providing downsizing services. In the latter capacity, he has worked with hundreds of executives who have had to make career transitions.

Mr. Double operated his own outplacement service in Chicago before becoming part owner and Executive Vice President for Redirections Inc., which provides executive assessment and coaching on a global basis to Fortune 100 firms. Redirections Inc. specializes in creating multiple rater assessment tools and coaching senior executives. Its client base includes multinational firms in virtually every industry in the United States, Korea, and Taiwan.

Acknowledgments

The following people made significant contributions to the publication of this book. Their efforts are both acknowledged and appreciated.

Sharyn Sweeney Bills
Freelance Writer
Glenview, IL

Reviewers

Janice Robertson
Policy Analyst
Department of Young Physician
  Services
American Medical Association

Carol Sprague
Senior Corporate Recruiter
Division of Employee Relations
  and Placement
American Medical Association

Staff

Suzanne Fraker
Product Line Director, Practice
  Management
Product Line Development
Book and Product Group

Jean Roberts
Managing Editor
Product Line Development
Book and Product Group

Tim Ryan
Marketing Manager
Sales and Marketing
Book and Product Group

Selby Toporek
Senior Communications
  Coordinator
Marketing Services
Book and Product Group

Contents

Introduction

"I assumed that if I could just get the best training and worked as hard as I could, everything would fall into place."

"I feel as though I have a career. It's just not the one I thought I was going to have."*

According to one forecast, the average American today can expect to work for ten different employers, keep each job 3.6 years, and change careers completely three times before retiring. Of course, those averages are not relevant to physicians. Or are they?

Once upon a time—say, ten years ago or so—the typical medical school graduate could easily envision the road he or she was likely to travel from the auditorium where medical degrees were conferred right to retirement's door. Some diversions from the path were not unlikely—a journey through academia, perhaps, or a side trip into public service. But for the most part, and for most physicians, completion of medical training lent an assurance about the professional future, real or perceived, and an expectation of a fairly predictable career.

Not so today. In the wake of the marketplace revolution known as managed care, and with rumblings of legislative health care "reform" still resonating, the only thing physicians seem able to count on today is constant change.

How will these changes affect your career? That's hard to say. But it seems likely that as change becomes a constant in health care, physicians will be moving into the American mainstream of career change and uncertainty in ever-increasing numbers.

*Quotes are from physician participants in American Medical Association (AMA) focus groups on career management.

The acquisition of medical training no longer implies a lifetime of work at the bedside or in the clinic. For every physician who adheres to the traditional path, increasingly more will be exercising the option of pursuing other courses. Some may feel forced to do so by circumstances. Others may understand that with accelerated change comes expanded opportunity, and gladly embrace the idea of professional and personal refreshment, renewal, and growth. Whatever the motivation, many more physicians than ever before are likely to experience the challenge of identifying and evaluating options and making career choices.

Taking charge of change

"I feel as though I'm being turned into a factory worker."

Many physicians perceive the changing health care environment as a threat. As the old certainties and old assurances vanish, feelings of helplessness and passivity are common. But negativism is neither warranted nor necessary. As a physician, you do have choices. You need not—indeed, you should not—wait for the moment when change is forced upon you. Career management, a concept well recognized in the business world, has equal relevance in the medical profession today. As the health care delivery system becomes ever more complex, possibilities expand for positioning and repositioning oneself within it. Nor are your options limited to those related to health care; an even wider world of opportunity may lie beyond that realm for those with appropriate interests and abilities.

The opportunity exists for you to steer your course toward your own personal and professional goals, not simply to be buffeted about by change. Through periodic review and analysis of important personal and professional indicators, any physician has the ability to design a more satisfying career, whether a new medical school graduate seeking to take that important first step into the professional world, a seasoned professional considering a mid-life change, or a long-time veteran contemplating the pros and cons of closing the books entirely on medical practice.

The tools by which to take control and manage your career are available to you, wherever you find yourself along the career path. This workbook will show you how to efficiently, effectively, and intelligently direct your efforts.

A word about the process: As you review the content of this workbook, please keep in mind what it is—and is not—intended to help you accomplish. It is a tool you can use to assess yourself and your current personal and professional situations. It can help you sort through possible options and weigh them against your personal preferences and attributes. It can even be used to help you assess the degree to which you are willing and able to weather the practical consequences of change, such as the impact on your personal life and on both your present and your future financial picture. This workbook is designed to help you clarify your thoughts and perhaps gain additional insights into yourself and the opportunities open to you. What it cannot—and is not intended to—do is to tell you exactly what job is the right job for you.

Consider this workbook a compass and not a map. It is designed to guide you through the first steps of what may be a long journey as you explore the possibility of career change. It cannot tell you exactly how to reach your final destination, but it should help point you in the right direction.

What is career management?

> *"Managing your career means being proactive and looking for opportunities. It means staying ahead of the curve so you can do the things you want to do, instead of the things you have to do."*

Career management—that's a new idea for a lot of physicians. If you can't count on faithfully following that familiar, traditional career path, what can you count on?

Well, you can count on change, and while that's a scary proposition for some physicians, others see it as the opportunity it really is. Because, believe it or not, you have more options than ever before. While some physicians focus on the negative aspects of change, others see the upside: as health care delivery becomes ever more complex, many new roles are being created. These roles must be filled, preferably by those who already know and understand the health care environment. And beyond health care, there's an even wider world of options to explore.

Of course, if you're satisfied with the status quo, if you're absolutely sure that you're in the right place and that nothing can come along to alter your situation, then you can relax and go with the flow. Or can you? Even in that case, don't you want to be open to new ideas, new opportunities, and the possibility of new experiences? Career management is the process that enables you to do just that: to keep both your options and your mind open.

Part I
What are your choices?

"There's no security. I'm not really sure I know what I'll be doing in five years."

Ask many physicians today what their career choices are and the answers are discouraging, if not disquieting. Caught up in the day-to-day demands of medical practice, attempting to navigate the bureaucratic labyrinths of insurance programs and managed care plans, many fail to see the opportunities that abound. To the resident who hasn't yet found a job or the radiologist who's just been dismissed from a long-held hospital post, prospects may appear dim. But you do have choices.

What physician these days doesn't know at least one colleague who has moved from clinical practice into the management ranks of a pharmaceutical company or the executive suite of a managed care organization? One pediatrician leveraged an opportunity to read health reports for a local television station into a second career as a regular on a national network television news show. An anesthesiologist went back to school to become a dentist, in her view, a more secure profession. A former oncologist is now happily contemplating the beauty of his newly acquired Colorado ranch. Another physician recently converted the value in his practice into several hundred acres of Vermont farmland.

Meanwhile, many physicians who have earned MBAs now regularly don three-piece suits instead of white coats. And, by one count, at least 2,000 others now have law degrees hanging next to their MDs.

But you don't need to go as far afield as television network news or the green acres of Vermont to benefit from a career management mentality. One report tells of an internist who finds relief from the stresses of modern medical practice in the half day each week he now devotes to painting. And many more physicians—especially, but not exclusively, women—are finding a better balance between professional and personal commitments through the process of analyzing their goals and actively designing a course by which to achieve them. For example, one plastic surgeon now limits her office practice to four days a week, devoting the fifth weekday exclusively to her family.

None of these life changes just happened, however. Each represents the culmination of a process of analysis, identification of options, and decision making that we call the career management process.

Indeed, whether your goal is to enhance your marketability as a physician, to examine the cost/benefit ratio of what you're getting out of your career in relation to what you're investing in it, or to explore the brave new world of possible alternative careers, you can better achieve it by applying basic career management techniques. You are neither helpless nor a victim. By becoming a physician in the first place, you have proven your ability to analyze a situation and arrive at an appropriate course of action. The same skills that you acquired to help patients can also be applied to helping yourself ensure not only survival in a constantly shifting universe but also a richer, fuller, and more rewarding life.

Options? Here are just a few that your colleagues are now pursuing:

Professional

- Research
- Teaching
- Hospital/managed care organization administration
- Sales or corporate management, especially within the pharmaceutical and medical supply industries
- Consulting, especially to insurance and law firms
- Medical public relations or journalism
- Turning personal interests (eg, financial management, art collecting, travel) into business enterprises
- Turning talents, passions, and skills (eg, cooking, woodworking, playing a musical instrument) into professional careers

Personal

- Changing specialties
- Reassessing values
- Relocating
- Reallocating work hours
- Redefining roles within the family
- Modifying lifestyle

Chapter One

Defining what you have to offer

"I'm stuck. I can't sing. I can't dance. I'm stuck."

You do have options, and you probably have more to offer than you're aware of. Consider the attributes that are common to physicians:

- Intelligence
- Reliability
- Responsibility
- Adaptability
- Energy
- Organizational skills
- Information-gathering skills
- Communications skills
- Problem-solving skills
- Time-management skills
- The ability to learn and continue learning
- The ability to work hard for long periods of time
- The ability to work well and make decisions under stress

In fact, if you've completed medical school, you've probably already risen to a challenge that few others are capable of meeting. And if you've practiced medicine successfully for even a few years, you've probably already acquired more creative, analytic, and management skills than most of the nation's workforce will ever achieve. Think about this: if you were hiring someone for any kind of job, wouldn't you like to have someone with your capabilities working for you?

Chapter Two

Identifying what stands in your way

"I'm too busy to think about managing my career."

If you have fears and concerns about your ability to plot and manage career change, you are not alone. In a series of focus groups held by the American Medical Association (AMA) in 1997, doctors themselves identified the major barriers they saw as hampering their ability to change the direction of their careers and lives. Here are some of the concerns they shared:

- I am overtrained and overqualified
- I am too old
- My financial requirements are too high
- I am too independent
- I am too ethical
- I am not a team player
- I have attitude or ego problems
- I lack humility
- I lack basic business skills
- I lack knowledge of the business world
- I can't afford financially to make a change
- I have too many family responsibilities to think of myself
- I have too many obligations
- It's too late for me to make a change

These are realistic concerns, but it's possible to turn some of these perceived negatives into positives, in your mind and in the job market. Are you overtrained—or capable of acquiring knowledge? Too old—or a mature, seasoned professional? Are you too independent—or a self-starter capable of working without direction? Do you lack humility—or are you confident of your abilities?

Yes, there may be practical barriers to overcome, such as financial issues and lack of skills other than those directly related to the practice of medicine. But these, after all, involve matters that lie within your control and ability to address.

But many doctors have larger issues to resolve, especially those for whom the question is not how to find a different path within the field of medicine, but whether more radical change may be in order.

Being a doctor means many things to physicians. Being a practicing physician is likely to be the source of personal satisfaction, prestige, power, and a certain type of lifestyle, not only for physicians but for those to whom they have obligations, as well. You have made a long, hard, and expensive investment in becoming who you are. Does contemplating change mean throwing that investment away?

As strongly as change may call to some, the prospect of leaving the bedside will elicit significant conflict and inner turmoil for others, turmoil that no series of exercises or simple rational process can possibly resolve. So be honest: making a career change may require more than being willing to modify the pattern of your daily life or the bottom line on your financial statements. It may drastically alter the way you view and value yourself.

When that is the case, it is essential to recognize and deal honestly and openly with whatever personal conflict the prospect of change may involve. You may need to learn more about yourself—how you think, feel, and act. Certain exercises that appear in the following pages are designed to help you identify fundamental issues and where potential conflicts may lie, but no book of this nature can provide the answers you'll need to address them. Fortunately, other resources are available to serve that purpose, including therapeutic support and career, family, and religious counseling. If the biggest barriers to change facing you lie within yourself or your family, you may want to avail yourself of those resources now.

Chapter Three

Discovering who you are

"I wake up some mornings and say, 'This is not what I had in mind.'"

Physician, know thyself. Self-knowledge is important, not because career management promises to help you satisfy every personal need or gratify every whim and desire, but because you will need a starting point, a touchstone, a fundamental scale by which you can weigh the options that you will find to be available to you.

For many, life happens, time passes, and it's only at some late date, if ever, that one takes stock of whether what one is doing really corresponds with who one is and what one values. But if you're going to take a more active role in shaping your destiny—and that, after all, is what career management is all about—then you need to be able to make rational choices. You need to be able to match the characteristics of each option against your personal profile of values and needs. The starting point is determining exactly what those values and needs are.

Begin by assessing some of the basic motivations that drive all human beings. Think carefully when choosing responses—they are the key to what really is and isn't important in life to you. And be sure to be totally honest. Remember, this is not a test. You will not be graded. And no one but you need ever see your responses.

Exercise 1
What matters most to me?

Rank each of the following values on a scale of 1 (least important to me) to 5 (most important to me)

	Ranking 1–5
Contributing to society	_____
Satisfying my personal needs	_____
Satisfying the needs of others	_____
Receiving the recognition of my colleagues	_____
Receiving recognition in the community	_____
Having the admiration of my family	_____
Having the admiration of friends	_____
Having self-respect	_____
Living comfortably enough to meet basic needs	_____
Living in a style that others would envy	_____
Supporting my family adequately	_____
Supporting my family lavishly	_____
Having job security	_____
Enjoying financial security	_____
Enjoying stability in life	_____
Enjoying continual intellectual stimulation	_____
Learning continually	_____
Being continually challenged	_____
Not having to continually prove myself	_____
Living stress-free	_____
Being considered adequate in my work	_____

Being considered outstanding in my work _____

Having a sense of purpose in my work _____

Interacting with others _____

Maintaining autonomy _____

Feeling a part of something _____

Enjoying independence _____

Fulfilling spiritual needs _____

Fulfilling financial needs _____

Fulfilling ego needs _____

Fulfilling social needs _____

Having a personal life that supports career demands _____

Being able to balance career and personal lives _____

Having adequate leisure time _____

Other _____ _____

_____ _____

_____ _____

Now review your responses. What patterns emerge? Are you primarily driven by a need for recognition or a desire for financial reward? Do you most seek the stimulation of challenge and striving for achievement, or is meeting personal needs of greater importance to you? Is it more important for you to earn the respect and admiration of others, or is achieving your own self-respect your greatest reward? Are you a social animal or an independent spirit? Of course, chances are that, if you're like the rest of us, both responses will apply to some degree. The objective in answering these questions is to identify which motivator is most important or significant for you.

Next, pick five of the motivators that are most important to you and list them here:

1. _____

2. _____

3. _____

4. _____

5. _____

Of these five, which must be satisfied within your career? Which can be satisfied in other ways? For example, if contributing to society is a primary motivator, is it possible that you could achieve that goal through volunteer work, as well as or instead of in your professional life?

Continue this evaluation process until you have a clearer picture in your mind of what you want and need your work to provide to you.

Reconciling conflicts

Undoubtedly, some of your key motivators will be in conflict with one another. Which of us, after all, doesn't want to have it all? Reexamine the list and identify any conflicts that may exist, then list the opposing motivators here:

This motivator: conflicts   **with this motivator:**

_____   _____

_____   _____

_____   _____

_____   _____

_____   _____

_____   _____

_____   _____

_____   _____

Now you must make choices and determine which motivator is of greater value to you. Adjust your rankings accordingly. Do the same top five still apply? If not, make the appropriate adjustment.

Exercise 2
What matters most in my work?

Let's change the focus now from the larger issues of what you want out of life to the more specific question of what you find most satisfying in your work. Review the following and check off the statements that apply to you.

I am most satisfied when I:

_____ Work as part of a team

_____ Work independently

_____ Supervise others

_____ Work under supervision

_____ Interact with others

_____ Compete with others

_____ Cooperate with others

_____ Work at my own pace

_____ Work under time pressure

_____ Follow established protocols and procedures

_____ Have to devise solutions to problems as they arise

_____ Have clearly defined responsibilities

_____ Have shifting responsibilities

_____ Have clearly defined work hours

_____ Establish my own work hours

_____ Can expect continuing satisfaction in my work

Am in a stable work situation, that is, one that is unlikely to change over the next five years

_____

Am in a dynamic work situation, that is, one that is likely to change over the next year or two

_____

Now that you have checked off those statements that indicate the things that are most important in work to you, identify the five that are most important and list them here:

1. _____

2. _____

3. _____

4. _____

5. _____

These five factors are likely to be the essentials that need to be present in your work if you are to find it satisfying.

Some conflicts may need to be reconciled, however. Let's say, for example, that you have indicated that both working as part of a team and competing with others are important to you. To resolve the apparent conflict, you would need to analyze what those statements mean to you. If your need for competition is satisfied when you compete as a team member with another team, there may be no conflict. If, on the other hand, you prefer to compete personally with other individuals, your needs may be in conflict.

When such conflicts become apparent, it is essential to consider what compromises, if any, you are willing to make. If you cannot reconcile such inconsistencies, you may be demanding the impossible from a work situation.

Chapter Four

Deciding if change is what you really want

"You just can't take job stability for granted anymore."

Nobody's life is perfect. We all know that, even though we probably all constantly dream of perfecting what we see as the imperfections of our existence. Certainly that's true of our work lives, which consume most of our waking hours. But change—especially career change—typically comes at a cost, a cost that may be measurable in terms of time, dollars, energy, effort, and emotional turmoil. So before you commit yourself to making those investments, it's important to be sure whether what you're trying to achieve is really worth what change will inevitably cost. Begin by making an objective assessment of your current situation.

Exercise 3
How satisfied/dissatisfied am I now?

In my current situation, I (check off those statements that apply to you):

_____ Contribute to society

_____ Satisfy my own personal needs

_____ Satisfy the needs of others

_____ Have the recognition of colleagues

_____ Have recognition in the community

_____ Have the admiration of my family

_____ Have the admiration of friends

_____ Enjoy self-respect

_____ Live comfortably enough to meet basic needs

_____ Live in a style others would envy

_____ Support my family adequately

_____ Support my family lavishly

_____ Have job security

_____ Enjoy financial security

_____ Experience challenge

_____ Experience continual intellectual stimulation

_____ Learn continually

_____ Am continually challenged

_____ Continually have to prove myself

_____ Live without stress

_____ Am considered adequate in my work

_____ Am considered outstanding in my work

_____ Have a sense of purpose in my work

_____ Interact with others

_____ Am autonomous

_____ Feel a part of something larger than myself

_____ Am independent

_____ Fulfill my spiritual needs

_____ Meet my financial needs

_____ Fulfill my ego needs

_____ Fulfill my social needs

_____ Have a personal life that accommodates the demands of my career

_____ Am able to balance career and personal lives

_____ Have adequate leisure time

Now let's do a similar exercise to determine the degree to which your current work situation corresponds to those things you find most satisfying.

Exercise 4
How satisfied/dissatisfied am I with my work?

My current work situation permits me to (check off the statements that apply to you):

_____ Supervise others

_____ Work free of supervision

_____ Work as a member of a team

_____ Work independently

_____ Interact with others

_____ Compete with others

_____ Cooperate with others

_____ Work at my own pace

_____ Work under time pressure

_____ Devise solutions

_____ Follow established protocols or procedures

_____ Set my own work hours

_____ Have clearly defined work hours

_____ Have clearly defined responsibilities

Now match your responses to the above two exercises with those on pages 10–11 and 13, in which you identified what matters most to you in life and what matters most in your work.

Next, returning to the list of what matters most to you in your life, assess the degree to which each of those factors is currently present or absent. In the following space list your primary motivators, that is, those that you ranked 4 or 5 in Exercise 1. Then indicate whether or not they are present in your current situation.

	Present	Absent

_____ ___ ___

_____ ___ ___

_____ ___ ___

_____ ___ ___

_____ ___ ___

_____ ___ ___

_____ ___ ___

_____ ___ ___

_____ ___ ___

_____ ___ ___

According to this assessment, is your current situation satisfying your primary motivators or drives? If not, where do the gaps lie? List them here:

_____

_____

_____

_____

_____

What's the bottom line? Is it time for a change?

Part II
What price change?

Let's assume indicators are that change would be desirable in your life. But as already noted, change does not come without a price. Are you—and those to whom you have obligations or with whom you have other types of bonds—ready to pay that price? Let's explore fully how change will impact your life and theirs.

First, consider how change will affect you.

Exercise 5
How will change affect me?

Check off the statements that apply to you.

Change may:

_____ Alter myself-image

_____ Alter how others view me

_____ Affect family relationships

_____ Affect other personal relationships

_____ Require financial sacrifice

_____ Mean loss of social status

_____ Mean loss of professional status

_____ Mean loss of standing in the community

_____ Require a change in lifestyle

_____ Disrupt established daily routines

_____ Mean abandoning the skills I've spent years developing

_____ Challenge my sense of self-confidence

_____ Undermine my sense of contributing to society

Now identify those changes that you would—and wouldn't—find acceptable.

I am willing to accept:

1. _____

2. _____

3. _____

4. _____

5. _____

I would find it difficult or impossible to accept:

1. _____

2. _____

3. _____

4. _____

5. _____

Obviously, there are no right or wrong answers to this exercise. Rather, it is intended to provide a focal point for identifying issues that may emerge as you embark upon a course that may lead to change.

What's the bottom line? Only you can make that call.

Chapter 5

Assessing your support system

No man or woman is an island, and chances are that you will not be the only person affected by any major life decisions you make. Spouses, children, other dependents, parents, and others may be among those affected by the choices you make. Certainly their needs, too, should be taken into account as you contemplate a career change.

Even more important, it is likely that you will need their full understanding and support, especially those of you who are considering changes that could have significant lifestyle and financial implications. Many a career change—and more than a marriage or two—have foundered when the commitment to change has not been fully shared. Therefore, it is strongly recommended that you explore essential issues and thoroughly air any differences in values or perceptions before you embark upon a course that may affect the significant others in your life to as great a degree as it will affect yours.

The following exercise is designed to help you and your spouse or other life partner identify the ways in which change may affect your relationship. Unlike previous exercises in this workbook, this exercise is to be completed by the person who will be directly affected by changes in your life. Ask that person to check off all of the statements that he or she believes would apply to him or her.

Exercise 6
How will change affect others?

Change may:

_____ Alter my self-image

_____ Alter how others view me

_____ Affect family relationships

_____ Affect other personal relationships

_____ Require financial sacrifice

_____ Mean loss of social status

_____ Mean loss of professional status

_____ Mean loss of standing in the community

_____ Require a change in lifestyle

_____ Disrupt established daily routines

Now ask your partner to identify those changes that he or she would—and wouldn't—find acceptable.

I am willing to accept:

1. _____

2. _____

3. _____

4. _____

5. _____

I would find it difficult or impossible to accept:

1. _____

2. _____

3. _____

4. _____

5. _____

It is hoped that, used as an opportunity to explore issues and expectations, completing the exercise will enable you and those to whom you have obligations identify the hidden hazards that may torpedo your expectations and aspirations. Remember, however, that this exercise is intended only to identify possible conflicts. But identifying issues is not tantamount to resolving them. It is strongly recommended that, should issues emerge that are not readily subject to resolution through discussion, additional support, such as religious or family counseling, be sought.

Others, of course, may also be affected by the possibility of a change in your work life. While it is impossible to anticipate all of the personal relationships that may be affected by changes in your career, it is strongly recommended that you ask anyone else whose life may be significantly affected by a change in your career to work through the same exercise.

Chapter Six

Analyzing the financial feasibility of change

"I'm just treading water, trying to keep my head above the surface."

What price change—literally? Can you afford it? Financially, where are you today? Where are you likely to be tomorrow if you attempt to adhere to the status quo? If a change in the direction of your career will affect income and expenses, how would the bottom line look? Let's begin answering those important questions by undertaking a complete survey of your current financial condition.

Worksheet 1
Current income and expenses

Income (or Cash Flow) Statement for the Most Recently Completed Tax Year

Income

Earned Income (Before Taxes)

    Salary, wages, practice net income

Husband	$	_____
Wife		_____
Bonus		_____
Self-employment income		_____
Annuities or pensions		_____
Social Security payment		_____
Other		_____
Earned income	$	_____

Investment Income

Interest	$	_____
Dividend		_____
Rental income		_____
Other		_____
Investment income	$	_____

Total Income (A) =　　　　　　$ _____

Expenses

Fixed Expenses

    Housing $ _____

    Utilities   _____

    Loan payments   _____

    Taxes

        Federal and state   _____

        Social Security   _____

        Property   _____

    Insurance premiums   _____

    Other   _____

    Fixed expenses $ _____

Variable Expenses

    Food $ _____

    Clothing   _____

    Travel/Recreation   _____

    Household maintenance   _____

    Transportation   _____

    Education   _____

    Medical expenses   _____

    Charity   _____

    Other   _____

    Variable expenses $ _____

Total Expenses (B) = $

Surplus/(Deficit) (A – B) = $ _____

Worksheet 2
Current net worth

Financial Condition as of (insert current date)

Assets

Current Assets

    Cash on hand $ _____

    Checking accounts   _____

    Savings accounts   _____

    Life insurance cash values   _____

    Stocks/Bonds   _____

    Mutual funds   _____

    Other   _____

        Subtotal $ _____

Real Estate/Investments

    Residences $ _____

    Rental income property   _____

    Real estate limited   _____

    Partnerships   _____

        Subtotal $ _____

Personal Assets

    Automobiles $ _____

    Household furnishings   _____

    Accessories   _____

    Jewelry, collections, etc   _____

    Other   _____

        Subtotal $ _____

Retirement Funds

    IRAs $ _____

    Salary savings (401k)   _____

    Vested pension benefits   _____

    Annuities   _____

    Other   _____

        Subtotal $ _____

    Total Assets (A) = $ _____

Liabilities

Current Liabilities (payment due within next 12 months)

    Unpaid bills $ _____

    Credit cards   _____

    Bank or installment loan   _____

    Resident mortgage loan   _____

    Other   _____

        Subtotal $ _____

Long-term Liabilities

    Bank or installment loan $ _____

    Resident mortgage loan   _____

    Other   _____

        Subtotal $ _____

    Total Liabilities (B) = $ _____

    Net Worth (A − B) = $ _____

Now assume that a career change you plan affects your income. Estimate what your income would be in the new circumstances. Complete Worksheets 3 and 4 accordingly. Then review your expenses carefully. Determine which, if any, you could and would modify in the event of a change in income. Remember: if the lifestyle of a spouse or others would be affected by these changes, be sure to include that person or persons in this review, as well. The time to identify sources of conflict over these sensitive issues is while they still remain theoretical.

Note: Of course, you may not be ready to perform this exercise at this time since it assumes that you already have a clear idea not only of what new course you will be pursuing but also of the remuneration you would receive. Those who are not yet ready to make a comparison of their present and possible financial situation should move ahead to Part III of this workbook. But keep in mind that this tool is available to you if and when the appropriate time to make such a comparison arrives.

Worksheet 3
Projected income and expenses

Assumed Income (or Cash Flow) Statement

Income

Earned Income (Before Taxes)

Salary, wages, practice net income _____

Husband $ _____

Wife _____

Bonus _____

Self-employment income _____

Annuities or pensions _____

Social Security payment _____

Other _____

Earned income $ _____

Investment Income

Interest $ _____

Dividend _____

Rental income _____

Other _____

Investment income $ _____

Total Income (A) = $ _____

Expenses

Fixed Expenses

    Housing $ _____

    Utilities   _____

    Loan payments   _____

    Taxes

        Federal and state   _____

        Social Security   _____

        Property   _____

    Insurance premiums   _____

    Other   _____

    Fixed expenses $ _____

Variable Expenses

    Food $ _____

    Clothing   _____

    Travel/Recreation   _____

    Household maintenance   _____

    Transportation   _____

    Education   _____

    Medical   _____

    Charity   _____

    Other   _____

    Variable expenses $ _____

Total Expenses (B) = $ _____

Surplus/(Deficit) (A – B) = $ _____

Next, consider how changes in annual income are likely to change your overall financial picture. Would you and those who would be affected by these changes be satisfied with what you see?

Worksheet 4
Projected net worth

Assets

Current Assets

    Cash on hand $ _____

    Checking accounts   _____

    Savings accounts   _____

    Life insurance cash values   _____

    Stocks/Bonds   _____

    Mutual funds   _____

    Other   _____

        Subtotal $ _____

Real Estate/Investments

    Residences $ _____

    Rental income property   _____

    Real estate limited   _____

    Partnerships   _____

        Subtotal $ _____

Personal Assets

    Automobiles $ _____

    Household furnishings   _____

    Accessories   _____

    Jewelry, collections, etc   _____

    Other   _____

        Subtotal $ _____

Retirement Funds

    IRAs $ _____

    Salary savings (401k)   _____

    Vested pension benefits   _____

    Annuities   _____

    Other   _____

        Subtotal $ _____

Total Assets (A) = $ _____

Liabilities

Current Liabilities (payment due within next 12 months)

    Unpaid bills $ _____

    Credit cards   _____

    Bank or installment loan   _____

    Residence mortgage loan   _____

    Other   _____

        Subtotal $ _____

Long-term Liabilities

    Bank or installment loan   _____

    Residence mortgage loan   _____

    Other   _____

        Subtotal   _____

Total Liabilities (B) = $ _____

Projected Net Worth (A – B) = $ _____

This is a good point at which to stop and evaluate what you've accomplished so far. Working through the preceding exercises, you have explored the possibility of making a change in your career, examining your motivations, values, and requirements. You have assessed the cost of change, psychological and financial, and begun to weigh whether what you would accomplish would be worth the price. You now should have a better understanding of yourself, what you want, what you need, and whatever barriers might stand in the way of realizing your objectives. It's time now to turn attention outward and consider more carefully what you have to work with to help you attain your goals.

Part III
Finding new direction

If you've come this far, chances are you've decided that you're not only ready but also willing and able to embrace change. But which way should you go? Where are you most likely to find success? What kinds of opportunities would you be wisest to avoid? To begin to answer those questions, let's determine where your basic strengths and weaknesses lie.

Chapter Seven

Identifying your basic skills

Exercise 7 describes eight basic skills sets: intellectual skills, administrative skills, personal impact skills, persuasive skills, accounting and financial skills, motivational skills, and personal skills. Consider each, thinking of concrete examples of when you have used them. In doing so, review the entire range of your experience, including the experiences you encountered in the course of your academic career, when performing volunteer activities, and in managing your personal affairs. Although your professional experience is, of course, significant in this assessment of basic skills, the objective is to think beyond the confines of that one dimension of your life and to review your total life experience. Your greatest strengths, after all, may lie in areas that you have not yet associated with possible career options.

Exercise 7
What are my basic skills?

As you identify relevant experiences, rate yourself in each of these areas according to how effective you are at using these skills. Rate yourself 3 for outstanding, 2 for adequate or average, and 1 for inadequate. As you complete rating yourself in each category, determine your average rating for that category.

Intellectual Skills

a. Judgment: the ability to use one's intelligence effectively, to make appropriate decisions, and to reach logical conclusions.   _____

b. Problem analysis: the ability to recognize the source of a problem.   _____

c. Creativity/innovativeness: the ability to come up with new solutions or apply old solutions in a new way.   _____

Average   _____

Administrative Skills

a. Planning and organizing: the ability to plan in advance.   _____

b. Coordination: the ability to coordinate resources to accomplish task objectives.   _____

c. Handling details: the ability to keep track of and remember many details important to getting a task done.   _____

d. Selecting personnel: the ability to choose the right person for a given task.   _____

e. Training personnel: the ability to train people to develop their full potential.   _____

f. Delegating: the ability to accomplish a task through subordinates or other persons.   _____

g. Managing controls: the ability to maintain control over processes to accomplish goals.   _____

h. Decision making: the ability to assimilate and organize information to arrive at an appropriate decision in a timely fashion.   _____

Average   _____

Interpersonal Skills

a. Oral communications: the ability to present material in an organized, interesting, articulate, and concise manner:

    In individual, face-to-face situations   _____

    In group situations   _____

b. Written communications: the ability to write clearly and in an organized, interesting, and appropriate manner.   _____

c. Human relations skills: empathy and responsiveness to the needs of others; the ability to develop trust and to take account of human relations factors in one's actions.   _____

Average   _____

Personal Impact Skills

a. Leadership: the ability to motivate a group to accomplish a task:

    With subordinates   _____

    With peers   _____

    With superiors   _____

b. Competitive assertiveness: the tendency to be assertive, forceful, and competitive in promoting one's own point of view or way of doing things:

    With subordinates   _____

    With peers   _____

    With superiors   _____

c. Impact: the ability to command respect, to show exceptional self-assurance, and to achieve personal recognition:

    With subordinates   _____

    With peers   _____

    With superiors   _____

d. Independence: the ability to plan actions based on one's own convictions.   _____

e. Managing conflict: the ability to resolve and reconcile conflicting views or forces.   _____

Average   _____

Persuasive Skills

a. Developing rapport: the ability to convince others to work in cooperation with you.   _____

b. Promotional/sales ability: the ability to promote a product or idea; the ability to sell tangible items.   _____

c. Selling intangibles: the ability to win acceptance of intangible ideas.   _____

Average   _____

Accounting and Financial Skills

a. Arithmetical skills: understanding of mathematical concepts and strong ability to compute and calculate with numbers or knowledge.   _____

b. Numerical reasoning: the ability to use numbers as a reasoning tool.   _____

c. Financial planning: the ability to devise an effective financial plan to achieve a given objective or outcome.   _____

d. Financial administration and control: the ability to prepare financial reports and control procedures.   _____

Average   _____

Motivational Skills

a. Work motivation: the tendency to see one's work as a central factor in life and as a major commitment in comparison with such competing activities as leisure, familial, or other personal pursuits. _____

b. Achievement drive: the desire to achieve significant goals at work, to respond to internally generated incentives to achievement; a constant desire to improve. _____

Average _____

Personal Skills

a. Resistance to stress: the ability to maintain appropriate and constructive responses in the face of unusual, surprising, or stressful circumstances. _____

b. Flexibility: the ability to adapt to the demands of different situations; the ability to modify plans and approaches in the face of changing circumstances. _____

c. Energy and physical stamina: the ability to meet the physical demands of a given work situation. _____

Average _____

Now you need at least two other points of view. The following exercise is intended for use by at least two persons who know you well and who can be trusted to be objective in helping you make this crucial analysis of strengths and weaknesses. Ideally, the individuals you select to perform this exercise will be drawn from two different realms in your life—a spouse and a long-time professional colleague, for example—so that the results will provide as well rounded a picture as possible. The major criteria in selecting participants, however, should be their knowledge of you and their willingness to objectively rate your skills and other attributes. (Of course, you may choose to ask more than two others to perform this rating. If you do, simply adapt the summary worksheet accordingly.)

Exercise 8
What are my basic skills? Objective analysis 1

Rating

Intellectual Skills

a. Judgment: the ability to use one's intelligence
    effectively, to make appropriate decisions, and to
    reach logical conclusions.   _____

b. Problem analysis: the ability to recognize the
    source of a problem.   _____

c. Creativity/innovativeness: the ability to come up with
    new solutions or apply old solutions in a new way.   _____

Average   _____

Administrative Skills

a. Planning and organizing: the ability to plan in
    advance and coordinate resources to accomplish
    task objectives.   _____

b. Coordination: the ability to coordinate resources
    to accomplish task objectives.   _____

c. Handling details: the ability to keep track of
    and remember many details important to getting
    a task done.   _____

d. Selecting personnel: the ability to choose the
    right person for a given task.   _____

e. Training personnel: the ability to train people to
    develop their full potential.   _____

f. Delegating: the ability to accomplish a task
    through subordinates or other persons.   _____

g. Managing controls: the ability to maintain
    control over processes to accomplish goals.   _____

h. Decision making: the ability to assimilate and
    organize information so as to arrive at an
    appropriate decision in a timely fashion.   _____

Average   _____

Assessing Your Career Options: A Workbook for Taking Charge of Change

Interpersonal Skills

a. Oral communications: the ability to present material in an organized, interesting, articulate, and concise manner:

 In individual, face-to-face situations   _____

 In group situations   _____

b. Written communications: the ability to write clearly and in an organized, interesting, and appropriate manner.   _____

c. Human relations skills: empathy and responsiveness to the needs of others; the ability to develop trust and to take account of human relations factors in one's actions.   _____

Average   _____

Personal Impact Skills

a. Leadership: the ability to motivate a group to accomplish a task:

 With subordinates   _____

 With peers   _____

 With superiors   _____

b. Competitive assertiveness: the tendency to be assertive, forceful, and competitive in promoting one's own point of view or way of doing things:

 With subordinates   _____

 With peers   _____

 With superiors   _____

c. Impact: the ability to command respect, to show exceptional self-assurance, and to achieve personal recognition:

With subordinates _____

With peers _____

With superiors _____

d. Independence: the ability to plan actions based on one's own convictions. _____

e. Managing conflict: the ability to resolve and reconcile conflicting views or forces. _____

Average _____

Persuasive Skills

a. Developing rapport: the ability to convince others to work in cooperation with you. _____

b. Promotional/sales ability: the ability to promote a product or idea; the ability to sell tangible items. _____

c. Selling intangibles: the ability to win acceptance of intangible ideas. _____

Average _____

Accounting and Financial Skills

a. Arithmetical skills: understanding of mathematical concepts and strong ability to compute and calculate with numbers or knowledge. _____

b. Numerical reasoning: the ability to use numbers as a reasoning tool. _____

c. Financial planning: the ability to devise an effective financial plan to achieve a given objective or outcome. _____

d. Financial administration and control: the ability to prepare financial reports and control procedures. _____

Average _____

Motivational Skills

a. Work motivation: the tendency to see one's work as a central factor in life and as a major commitment in comparison with such competing activities as leisure, familial, or other personal pursuits.   _____

b. Achievement drive: the desire to achieve significant goals at work, to respond to internally generated incentives to achievement; a constant desire to improve.   _____

Average   _____

Personal Skills

a. Resistance to stress: the ability to maintain appropriate and constructive responses in the face of unusual, surprising, or stressful circumstances.   _____

b. Flexibility: the ability to adapt to the demands of different situations; the ability to modify plans and approaches in the face of changing circumstances.   _____

c. Energy and physical stamina: the ability to meet the physical demands of a given work situation.   _____

Average   _____

What are my basic skills? Objective analysis 2

Rating

Intellectual Skills

a. Judgment: the ability to use one's intelligence effectively, to make appropriate decisions, and to reach logical conclusions.   _____

b. Problem analysis: the ability to recognize the source of a problem.   _____

c. Creativity/innovativeness: the ability to come up with new solutions or apply old solutions in a new way.   _____

Average   _____

Administrative Skills

a. Planning and organizing: the ability to plan in advance.   _____

b. Coordination: the ability to coordinate resources to accomplish task objectives.   _____

c. Handling details: the ability to keep track of and remember many details important to getting a task done.   _____

d. Selecting personnel: the ability to choose the right person for a given task.   _____

e. Training personnel: the ability to train people to develop their full potential.   _____

f. Delegating: the ability to accomplish a task through subordinates or other persons.   _____

g. Managing controls: the ability to maintain control over processes to accomplish goals.   _____

h. Decision making: the ability to assimilate and organize information so as to arrive at an appropriate decision in a timely fashion.   _____

Average   _____

Interpersonal Skills

a. Oral communications: the ability to present material in an organized, interesting, articulate, and concise manner:

   In individual, face-to-face situations   _____

   In group situations   _____

b. Written communications: the ability to write clearly and in an organized, interesting, and appropriate manner.   _____

c. Human relations skills: empathy and responsiveness to the needs of others; the ability to develop trust and to take account of human relations factors in one's actions.   _____

Average   _____

Personal Impact Skills

a. Leadership: the ability to motivate a group to accomplish a task:

    With subordinates   _____

    With peers   _____

    With superiors   _____

b. Competitive assertiveness: the tendency to be assertive, forceful, and competitive in promoting one's own point of view or way of doing things:

    With subordinates   _____

    With peers   _____

    With superiors   _____

c. Impact: the ability to command respect, to show exceptional self-assurance, and to achieve personal recognition:

    With subordinates   _____

    With peers   _____

    With superiors   _____

d. Independence: the ability to plan actions based on one's own convictions.   _____

e. Managing conflict: the ability to resolve and reconcile conflicting views or forces.   _____

Average   _____

Persuasive Skills

a. Developing rapport: the ability to convince others
to work in cooperation with you.   _____

b. Promotional/sales ability: the ability to promote a
product or idea; the ability to sell tangible items. _____

c. Selling intangibles: the ability to win acceptance
of intangible ideas.   _____

Average   _____

Accounting and Financial Skills

a. Arithmetical skills: understanding of mathematical
concepts and strong ability to compute and calculate
with numbers or knowledge.   _____

b. Numerical reasoning: the ability to use numbers
as a reasoning tool.   _____

c. Financial planning: the ability to devise an effective
financial plan to achieve a given objective or outcome. _____

d. Financial administration and control: the ability to
prepare financial reports and control procedures.   _____

Average   _____

Motivational Skills

a. Work motivation: the tendency to see one's work
as a central factor in life and as a major commitment
in comparison with such competing activities as
leisure, familial, or other personal pursuits.   _____

b. Achievement drive: the desire to achieve significant
goals at work, to respond to internally generated
incentives to achievement; a constant desire to improve. _____

Average   _____

Personal Skills

a. Resistance to stress: the ability to maintain appropriate and constructive responses in the face of unusual, surprising, or stressful circumstances.   _____

b. Flexibility: the ability to adapt to the demands of different situations; the ability to modify plans and approaches in the face of changing circumstances.   _____

c. Energy and physical stamina: the ability to meet the physical demands of a given work situation.   _____

Average   _____

Now that you and at least two other persons have rated you in these eight basic skill sets, it's time to put all the pieces together. The exercise is a simple one.

Exercise 9
Summing up: A skills assessment

In the columns below, fill in the average rate arrived at by each assessor of your skills and then average those ratings to arrive at a composite view. (Remember to adjust this worksheet by adding additional columns if you've asked more than two persons to provide an objective analysis.)

Skill	Ratings			
	Self	First Analyst	Second Analyst	Average Rating
Intellectual Skills				
Judgment	_____	_____	_____	_____
Problem analysis	_____	_____	_____	_____
Creativity/innovativeness	_____	_____	_____	_____
Administrative Skills				
Planning and organizing	_____	_____	_____	_____
Coordination	_____	_____	_____	_____
Handling details	_____	_____	_____	_____
Selecting personnel	_____	_____	_____	_____
Training personnel	_____	_____	_____	_____
Delegating	_____	_____	_____	_____
Managing controls	_____	_____	_____	_____
Decision making	_____	_____	_____	_____
Interpersonal Skills				
Oral communications	_____	_____	_____	_____
Face-to-face	_____	_____	_____	_____
In groups	_____	_____	_____	_____
Written communications	_____	_____	_____	_____
Human relations	_____	_____	_____	_____

Skill	Ratings		
	Self	**First Analyst**	**Second Analyst**	**Average Rating**

Skill	Self	First Analyst	Second Analyst	Average Rating
Personal Impact Skills				
Leadership	_____	_____	_____	_____
Competitive assertiveness	_____	_____	_____	_____
Impact	_____	_____	_____	_____
Independence	_____	_____	_____	_____
Managing conflict	_____	_____	_____	_____
Persuasive Skills				
Developing rapport	_____	_____	_____	_____
Promotional/sales ability	_____	_____	_____	_____
Selling intangibles	_____	_____	_____	_____
Accounting and Financial Skills				
Arithmetical skills	_____	_____	_____	_____
Numerical reasoning	_____	_____	_____	_____
Financial planning	_____	_____	_____	_____
Financial administration and control	_____	_____	_____	_____
Motivational Skills				
Work motivation	_____	_____	_____	_____
Achievement drive	_____	_____	_____	_____
Personal Skills				
Resistance to stress	_____	_____	_____	_____
Flexibility	_____	_____	_____	_____
Energy and physical stamina	_____	_____	_____	_____

Chapter Eight

Learning from life's experiences

In addition to your self-analysis of strengths and weaknesses and the insights of those you have chosen to perform the same exercise, there is another important source of information to tap in objectively assessing the materials you would have to work with in implementing a career change: the full range of your life's experiences. Considered carefully, your life experiences have a great deal to tell you about the kinds and types of accomplishments you're capable of, helping you further define your greatest assets and perhaps even pointing to career directions you've not yet even considered.

Start by reviewing your life and listing ten instances in which you accomplished something that was a source of particular pride or satisfaction—personal, professional, or both. Again, be sure to go back and review your total life experience, calling upon instances drawn from every realm of life: academic, personal, and social, as well as professional. Remember, you are the sum total of all those experiences, so stretch your thinking as broadly as you can.

Exercise 10
What are my major accomplishments?

Example: As a college student, I maintained an A- grade average while working 25 hours a week as a shoe salesperson to defray college expenses.

1. _____

   _____

   _____

2. _____

   _____

   _____

3. _____

   _____

   _____

4. _____

   _____

   _____

5. _____

   _____

   _____

6. _____

   _____

   _____

7. _____

   _____

   _____

8. _____

_____

_____

9. _____

_____

_____

10. _____

_____

_____

Now, analyze each of those accomplishments to identify which resources, skills, or abilities you drew upon in achieving them. Think through each experience carefully to identify every component that contributed to its successful or satisfying outcome.

Example:

1. Major accomplishment:

As a college student, I maintained an A- grade average while
working 25 hours a week as a shoe salesperson to defray
college expenses.

Resources, skills, abilities demonstrated:
Sufficient intellect to achieve high academic standing
Resourcefulness in identifying means to meet financial needs
Persuasive skills to succeed as a salesperson
Sufficient stamina to maintain demanding schedule
Goal-orientedness

Now apply the same analysis to each of your major accomplishments.

1. Major accomplishment:

    _____

    _____

    _____

    Resources, skills, abilities demonstrated:

    _____

    _____

    _____

    _____

    _____

    _____

    _____

    _____

2. Major accomplishment:

    _____

    _____

    _____

    Resources, skills, abilities demonstrated:

    _____

    _____

    _____

    _____

    _____

    _____

    _____

3. Major accomplishment:

_____

_____

_____

Resources, skills, abilities demonstrated:

_____

_____

_____

_____

_____

_____

_____

_____

4. Major accomplishment:

_____

_____

_____

Resources, skills, abilities demonstrated:

_____

_____

_____

_____

_____

_____

_____

5. Major accomplishment:

_____

_____

_____

Resources, skills, abilities demonstrated:

_____

_____

_____

_____

_____

_____

_____

6. Major accomplishment:

_____

_____

_____

Resources, skills, abilities demonstrated:

_____

_____

_____

_____

_____

_____

_____

7. Major accomplishment:

    _____

    _____

    _____

    Resources, skills, abilities demonstrated:

    _____

    _____

    _____

    _____

    _____

    _____

    _____

8. Major accomplishment:

    _____

    _____

    _____

    Resources, skills, abilities demonstrated:

    _____

    _____

    _____

    _____

    _____

    _____

    _____

    _____

    _____

9. Major accomplishment:

_____

_____

_____

Resources, skills, abilities demonstrated:

_____

_____

_____

_____

_____

_____

_____

10. Major accomplishment:

_____

_____

_____

Resources, skills, abilities demonstrated:

_____

_____

_____

_____

_____

_____

_____

_____

By now, some clear patterns should have emerged, telling you where your greatest strengths and abilities lie. Based on the three previous exercises—your self-analysis of strengths and weaknesses, the analyses of others, and your review of your most positive life experiences—list below your greatest skills and major assets.

The skills that I and others agree are the strongest:

_____

_____

_____

_____

_____

_____

_____

_____

The accomplishments that demonstrate those skills:

_____

_____

_____

_____

_____

_____

_____

_____

These are the building blocks with which to construct your future.

Chapter Nine

Defining your ideal job

In working through the previous exercises, you've undoubtedly invested a considerable amount of effort and energy in reviewing past performance and analyzing what those experiences tell you about yourself. Now switch gears for a moment and undertake an exercise that demands little more than letting your imagination take flight. Consider all the options that life might afford you, try them on for size, and see how they feel. The purpose of this exercise isn't to exactly define which career niche you fit into; rather, it's to help open your mind and expand your thinking about possibilities.

Exercise 10
What on-the-job activities do I prefer to perform?

In this exercise, rank the following activities on a scale of 1 to 5, 1 representing the activities you'd least like to perform on the job and 5 those you'd most like to perform.

	Rank
Logical/Mathematical Activities	
Assemble or build technical equipment	_____
Collect things such as stamps, coins, cards, art, etc	_____
Design technical equipment	_____
Perform electrical wiring and repairs	_____
Operate electronic equipment	_____
Operate keyboard equipment	_____
Operate scientific equipment for instruction, experiments, or other purposes	_____

Read about and analyze historical events   _____

Read about technological developments   _____

Read medical or scientific journals   _____

Record accurately such things as numbers, membership
lists, sports statistics, scientific observations   _____

Repair electronic equipment, such as computers,
television sets, radios, etc   _____

Repair mechanical equipment, such as cars, engines, etc   _____

Use math for work, study, research, or other activities   _____

Work in science-related fields, such as animal science,
wildlife, or archeology   _____

Linguistic Activities

Announce radio or television programs   _____

Belong to a literary or book club   _____

Do crossword puzzles   _____

Edit a professional publication   _____

Edit the writings of my peers or others   _____

Learn a foreign language   _____

Perform in a show   _____

Persuade others to my point of view   _____

Prepare and present speeches to groups of people   _____

Read books, magazines, and newspapers   _____

Recite poetry to an audience   _____

Use accurate grammar, punctuation, spelling, and
grammatical structure when writing   _____

Use my imagination to find new ways to do or
say something   _____

Write clearly   _____

Write for a professional publication _____

Write poetry _____

Write short stories or plays _____

Write the words to music _____

Visual/Spatial Activities

Build cabinets or furniture _____

Carve figures of people, animals, or scenes _____

Create lighting effects for stages or studios _____

Design and build scenery for stages or studios _____

Design and landscape a flower garden _____

Design clothes or costumes _____

Design artwork _____

Design or help to build objects like models, rooms,
and home additions _____

Develop, edit, and work with film for photography
or video _____

Draw portraits, landscapes, and other pictures _____

Judge distance, speed, and movement of objects or people _____

Make drawings of machines or other mechanical
equipment _____

Paint portraits, landscapes, and other scenes _____

Plan arrangement of advertising materials _____

Read blueprints _____

Read complicated schematics _____

Sculpt a statue or other works of art _____

Take photographs _____

Use computer graphics in design _____

Musical Activities

Compose or arrange music   _____

Conduct an orchestra   _____

Create dance routines   _____

Perform dance routines   _____

Play a musical instrument solo or in a band or orchestra   _____

Sing solo or in a chorus or other group   _____

Take ballet or other dance lessons   _____

Take singing lessons   _____

Take lessons in playing a musical instrument   _____

Write songs for plays   _____

Body Kinesthetic Activities

Act in a play   _____

Build model airplanes, automobiles, or boats   _____

Camp, hike, or engage in other outdoor activities   _____

Construct stage sets for theatrical productions   _____

Do a pantomime, using body movements and facial expressions   _____

Do impersonations   _____

Do needlework   _____

Hunt or target shoot   _____

Install and repair home stereo equipment   _____

Juggle   _____

Make belts or other leather articles   _____

Make ceramic objects   _____

Model clothing for a designer, department store, or fashion show   _____

Mount and frame pictures   _____

Operate any motor-driven vehicle for pleasure or work, including cars, trucks, vans, boats, airplanes, tractors, or similar equipment _____

Paint the interior or exterior of houses or buildings _____

Perform work requiring substantial physical activity _____

Practice and participate in sports _____

Refinish or reupholster furniture _____

Repair or assemble mechanical devices, medical equipment, or specialized tools _____

Swim for recreation or competition _____

Take lessons in martial arts _____

Trim shrubs and hedges _____

Use tools such as pliers, wrenches, hammers, saws, or power tools _____

Use hands or hand tools _____

Weave rugs or make quilts _____

Work to develop muscles, flexibility, strength, or relaxation through massage, physical therapy, or strength training _____

Interpersonal Activities

Act as a tutor or counselor _____

Develop good relationships with others _____

Direct or supervise the activities of others _____

Get others to buy something or to agree with my ideas _____

Help others learn something of interest to them _____

Lead a group _____

Meet and talk with people _____

Plan events _____

Serve the needs of customers _____

Train dogs or other animals _____

Understand the behaviors of animals and use this
knowledge to work with them   _____

Understand the behaviors of people and use this
knowledge to work with them   _____

Intrapersonal Characteristics

Accept full responsibility for managing an activity   _____

Accept the risk of physical injury   _____

Adjust to the physical and mental pressures of competition   _____

Change work assignments and duties frequently   _____

Concentrate on tasks for long periods of time   _____

Cope with interruptions   _____

Demonstrate poise and confidence while performing
before an audience and under pressure   _____

Follow instructions, rules, or laws without close
supervision   _____

Follow training rules strictly   _____

Make decisions based on my personal experience
and opinions   _____

Finally, list here all the activities that you've ranked a 5 and see what
patterns emerge.

_____

_____

_____

_____

_____

_____

_____

_____

Now narrow the field by looking at some of the factors that may or may not be important to you in a job.

Exercise 11
What are my job requirements?

Rank the following on a scale of 1 to 5, 1 representing the factors that are least important to you and 5 those that are most important to you.

	Rank
A job that:	
Requires creativity	_____
Permits me to follow established routines	_____
Permits flexibility in the work schedule	_____
Requires a great deal of interpersonal interaction	_____
Permits a great deal of independent action	_____
Permits me to influence others	_____
Provides a great deal of intellectual stimulation	_____
Requires a great deal of improvisation	_____
Provides status and prestige	_____
Gives me power over others	_____
Is free of responsibility for others	_____
Pays a high salary	_____
Provides good benefits	_____
Provides a great deal of recognition	_____
Requires risk taking	_____
Is risk-free	_____
Requires frequent travel	_____
Requires no travel	_____
Demands performance under pressure	_____

Is stress-free   _____

Requires competition with others   _____

Requires cooperation with others   _____

What's most important to you? List the job attributes you've
ranked 5 here:

_____

_____

_____

_____

_____

_____

_____

_____

Given the job activities and attributes you've identified as most
important to you, describe your ideal job and work situation here:

_____

_____

_____

_____

_____

_____

_____

_____

Chapter Ten

Measuring your managerial potential

In the ever-expanding world of managed care, career change for many physicians will mean moving from the bedside to the managerial ranks of a health care plan or institution. Certainly, given the increasing recognition of the need to more effectively manage the delivery of health care, that is where many new job opportunities will lie. But the management of health care requires a far different mind-set and skill sets than does the direct delivery of patient care. Before joining the rush to the nearest business school, it's worth taking a careful look at exactly where your aptitudes, interests, and inclinations lie. (If you have no interest in considering this career change option, you may proceed directly to Chapter 12. However, keep in mind that many work situations require at least some degree of managerial skill, so there may be value in working through this exercise, even if your eye is not on a corporate front office.)

The following exercise, adapted from a self-assessment tool designed for managerial personnel, may provide some insight into how comfortably you would feel—and how well you might fare—in a managerial role. Again, in completing this exercise, consider your whole life experience, including not only your practice management skills but also those that you've exercised participating in volunteer activities, managing personal affairs, and so on. With just a little creative thinking, you should be able to project yourself into, and assess your potential competence in, a managerial role.

Exercise 12
What is my managerial potential?

When considering the success factors identified below, think of
concrete examples of when you have utilized the identified skills.
Then rate yourself on how effectively you believe you have used these
skills, using a scale of 1 to 5, 5 representing outstanding performance;
4, better than average performance; 3, average performance; 2, below
average performance; and 1, inadequate performance.

Success Factor 1: Strategic Focus

Gathers many different kinds of information and uses a wide variety
of sources to build a rich informational environment for the organization. Builds frameworks or models; forms concepts, hypotheses,
or ideas on the basis of information; becomes aware of patterns,
trends, and cause/effect relationships. Generates new ideas, brings
perspective and approaches together and combines them in creative
ways. Freely and regularly shares business and strategic information
throughout the organization.

Rating

1. Thinks globally:

    a. Gathers information from a broad range of
        internal and external sources in preparation
        for decision making   _____

    b. Builds an information-rich environment for
        the organization   _____

    c. Bases planning on thorough understanding of
        relevant data   _____

    d. Stays abreast of global trends that could have
        an impact on the business (eg, political, social,
        cultural, legal)   _____

    e. Recognizes opportunities for expansion and
        strategic alliances   _____

2. Analyzes issues:

    a. Understands complex concepts and relationships   _____

    b. Uses logical, analytical approaches to
       conceptualize problems   _____

    c. Analyzes problems from different points of view   _____

    d. Effectively evaluates pros and cons of different
       options   _____

    e. Searches for patterns, trends, and relationships to
       identify problems   _____

3. Innovates:

    a. Generates innovative and creative solutions
       to problems   _____

    b. Fosters innovative approaches to problem
       solving in others   _____

    c. Creatively integrates ideas and perspectives
       of others   _____

4. Communicates vision:

    a. Conveys a sense of mission that captures the
       imagination of others   _____

    b. Communicates clearly about the future of the
       organization   _____

    c. Communicates business strategy to all levels of
       the organization   _____

    d. Keeps people informed about issues impacting
       their jobs   _____

Success Factor 2: Results Orientation

Possesses high internal work standards and sets ambitious, yet attainable, goals. Persists in the face of adversity. Aligns tasks with strategic priorities. Structures the task for the team. Implements plans and ideas. Unhesitatingly makes decisions as required. Handles everyday work challenges with confidence and is able to adjust to multiple demands, shifting priorities, and rapid changes.

Rating

1. Drives for results:

    a. Persists in achieving goals when faced with obstacles _____

    b. Conveys an appropriate sense of urgency _____

    c. Makes tough decisions when necessary _____

    d. Makes timely decisions _____

    e. Acts decisively _____

2. Aligns strategy and planning

    a. Establishes direction within area of responsibility that is consistent with the overall corporate mission _____

    b. Translates strategic perspective into pragmatic action plans _____

    c. Clearly defines roles and expectations of direct reports/other team members _____

    d. Allocates resources to tasks according to strategic priorities _____

    e. Maximizes use of available resources _____

3. Demonstrates adaptability/flexibility:

    a. Identifies feasible alternatives or multiple options in planning and decision making _____

    b. Anticipates problems and develops contingency plans _____

   c. Monitors progress of others and redirects efforts
      when appropriate   _____

   d. Communicates to supervisors when corporate
      focus should change   _____

   e. Recognizes when it is time to shift strategic
      direction   _____

Success Factor 3: Leadership of Change

Driven to do things better, to improve, to be more effective and efficient. Measures progress against targets. Takes bold actions to move the organization forward; expresses confidence in the future of the actions to be taken. Challenges the status quo. States own "stand" on issues and commits self and others, accordingly.

Rating

1. Champions continuous improvement:

   a. Supports new business initiatives   _____

   b. Takes responsibility for initiating necessary change   _____

   c. Champions positive changes within the organization _____

   d. Develops structures and processes to support change _____

   e. Prepares people to understand change   _____

2. Leads courageously:

   a. Demonstrates principled leadership and ethical
      behavior   _____

   b. Demonstrates willingness to express unpopular
      points of view   _____

   c. Appropriately challenges higher level management   _____

   d. Supports risk taking by others   _____

   e. Takes appropriate business risks   _____

Success Factor 4: Leadership of People

Creates a positive environment in which others increase their awareness of their own strengths and limitations; provides coaching, training, and developmental resources to improve performance. Creates a sense of excitement; inspires a feeling of personal investment. Creates an environment where people perform beyond their own expectations. Inspires the confidence and trust of others. Takes responsibility for all aspects of the situation and for the success and failure of the group. Empowers others to achieve.

Rating

1. Attracts and develops talent:

    a. Builds teams whose members have diverse and complementary strengths   _____

    b. Provides challenging developmental opportunities for people   _____

    c. Provides direct/clear feedback when performance standards are met   _____

    d. Provides direct/constructive feedback when performance standards are not met   _____

2. Motivates others:

    a. Inspires a sense of excitement and personal investment in the overall success of the organization   _____

    b. Sets high standards of performance for others   _____

    c. Rewards achievement based on performance and competence   _____

    d. Creates an environment in which people perform beyond their own expectations   _____

    e. Celebrates significant organizational achievements   _____

3. Inspires confidence:

   a. Inspires the confidence and trust of others   _____

   b. Takes responsibility for own actions   _____

   c. Takes responsibility for the actions of own
      department or organization   _____

   d. Shows consistency between words and behavior   _____

   e. Delivers on commitments   _____

4. Empowers others:

   a. Accurately assesses the skill level of others   _____

   b. Provides others necessary information and
      support to carry out their responsibilities   _____

   c. Provides others sufficient authority to carry out
      their responsibilities   _____

   d. Reduces the obstacles that hinder performance
      of others   _____

   e. Empowers others to initiate tasks or projects they
      think are important   _____

Success Factor 5: Coalition Building

Treats others with respect; develops effective work relationships. Encourages the open expression of ideas. Comprehends events, issues, and opportunities from the viewpoint of others. Involves others and is able to build cooperative teams in which group members feel valued and empowered and have shared goals. Manages conflict situations effectively. Uses a variety of methods (eg, persuasive arguments, modeling behavior, and forming alliances) to gain support for ideas, strategies, and values.

1. Builds relationships:

    a. Develops effective relationships with higher management   _____

    b. Develops effective relationships with direct reports   _____

    c. Develops effective relationships with peers   _____

    d. Effectively represents company in outside relationships (eg, security analysts, community agencies, customers)   _____

    e. Conveys respect and appreciation for people with different backgrounds and experiences   _____

2. Fosters teamwork:

    a. Fosters development of a common vision across teams   _____

    b. Recognizes team accomplishments   _____

    c. Discourages turf behavior between different work groups   _____

    d. Integrates planning efforts across teams   _____

3. Negotiates and influences internally:

    a. Addresses conflict situations directly   _____

    b. Expresses disagreement in ways that communicate respect and understanding of others' points of view   _____

    c. Presents arguments in ways that win the support of others   _____

Success Factor 6: Personal Impact

Presents ideas clearly, with ease and interest, so that the other person (or audience) understands what is being communicated. Seeks feedback and modifies behavior in response to feedback; understands own strengths and weaknesses. Strives to balance work and personal lives.

Rating

1. Communicates clearly:

   a. Presents ideas clearly and concisely   _____

   b. Shapes presentation of ideas to meet audience needs   _____

2. Models self-development:

   a. Continually works to improve professional skills   _____

   b. Seeks feedback from others on performance   _____

   c. Acts on feedback from others   _____

   d. Understands and compensates for own limitations   _____

   e. Maintains a sense of humor   _____

Success Factor 7: Industry Depth

Understands what it takes to be successful in the industry. Has broad knowledge of the industry's history and current trends; understands its technologies, markets, customers, and competitors. Applies market insights and industry knowledge to strategy development. Understands the implications of key financial indicators.

Rating

1. Applies market, customer, and technical knowledge:

   a. Displays a thorough understanding of the industry's current environment (including regulations, markets, customers, competitors, growth trends, etc)   _____

   b. Applies knowledge of the competition's strengths and weaknesses to develop internal strategy   _____

   c. Anticipates customer needs and/or requirements   _____

    d. Develops personal agenda consistent with
        customer needs   _____

    e. Focuses the organization on efforts that add
        value to the customer   _____

2. Demonstrates financial acumen:

    a. Incorporates understanding of key financial
        indicators in planning process   _____

    b. Accurately forecasts market impact on the
        organization's financial performance   _____

    c. Builds an inventory of issues and selects accurately
        the customer's limitations financially, tactically,
        and with systems   _____

    d. Applies understanding of business financials to
        solve customer problems   _____

3. Negotiates effectively with customers:

    a. Brings the customer to closure on specific strategies
        and tactics for business development   _____

    b. Develops closing opportunities consistent with
        customer needs   _____

    c. Establishes monitoring process to ensure attainment
        of customer goals   _____

Moving from bedside to desk is a major step. Completion of this exercise should provide some insight into your managerial potential, as well as help you identify where your strengths and development needs may lie if playing a leadership role within an organizational structure is among the career options you are considering.

Chapter Eleven

What do you have to offer? A reality check

As a result of working through the previous exercises, and with the help of those who you have asked to provide additional insight through the completion of the exercises on pages 24 and 46, you now have taken a long, hard look at yourself. You have a sense of your strengths and preferences, and you have some idea of what to avoid and what gaps in your background, experience, and/or skills may need to be filled. You also should have identified what you would find most satisfying in a work situation. Where to go from here?

Again, let your imagination reign. Think of your ideal job or work situation. Then pretend that you are applying for that position and draft a letter to your potential employer outlining your qualifications. Here are some examples to help stimulate your thinking.

Dear _____ :

In an ad in the March 1997 *Journal of XYZ* for a Director of Clinic Assays, your firm recently indicated its interest in recruiting an innovative leader who has experience leading teams in high-pressure situations.

As a professor of research techniques at ABC Medical School for the past ten years, I have taught in the most demanding discipline of research: testing drug therapies for human trials. These assignments were often in conjunction with Food and Drug Administration guidelines and restrictions. The published outcomes always generated great interest.

My career thus far has been fulfilling but not quite as challenging as I would like it to be. My team leadership abilities are most often at the back end of discoveries rather than at the cutting edge. While leading the brightest of student practitioners and overseeing the design of the clinical processes is always exciting, I have been interested in moving beyond this domain into a more challenging one.

For some time I have been looking seriously at industry as the best alternative for me. Therefore, I would welcome the opportunity to explore the position outlined in your ad, or other related roles that would draw upon the skills that I have to offer as:

Team-oriented leader and coach
Bottom line manager, pragmatic and thorough
Innovator, creative thinker, and problem solver
Communicator, both verbally and in writing
Visionary leader who grew the school's business 500 percent in
    ten years
Manager with excellent interpersonal skills coupled with political savvy

The enclosed resume provides more details.

I will contact you soon in follow-up to this letter.

Sincerely,

Dear Dr. _____ :

I have followed your company's growth and progress over the past five years with great interest, which stems from my own background in designing medical tools and techniques that require the use of those tools.

Your company has been at the forefront of manufacturing and selling new tools to medical practitioners. Your sales group and engineers have been invited by my organization, All American Hospital, to display your product line and to help us learn how best to use these utensils. More importantly, my colleagues inform me that your company actively pursues new ideas and often supports the development of such items.

I am writing to you because, while I have had a successful medical practice for the past ten years, I have found myself in recent years devoting more of my time and research abilities to developing new tools in the cardiovascular field. Some of these have proven quite useful. My accompanying resume highlights some of these achievements.

I have a strong interest in leading research and development within my practice area for an organization with a proven track record in getting high-quality innovative products into the field. I would welcome the opportunity to meet with you or your representatives to discuss that interest.

I will call you soon in the hope that our interest in pursuing this possibility might be mutual.

Sincerely,

What have you learned in drafting your letter? Do the attributes, skills, and experience you have translate into those that would be required by the job? You may, indeed, find that you are more qualified than you might have expected. If you're not fully qualified yet, you may consider one or two choices:

- *Plan 1:* Identify the gaps and develop a plan to fill them.
- *Plan 2:* Abandon this career option and develop another to take its place, then test its feasibility using the same process.

The choice is yours.

The next step:
Taking action

The opening pages of this workbook emphasized an important point: physicians have more options than ever before. Now, having worked through the preceding pages, you have already identified the essential issues and answered the important questions that must be addressed if you are to take advantage of those options. You should know whether or not you're really ready for change and, if so, what potential barriers might stand in your way. You've considered the financial implications and assessed the strength of your support system. You've systematically identified your strengths and weaknesses in the world of work and clearly defined what you hope to find there. You should know what you want to do, why you want to do it, and what skills you can bring to the table. So far, you're off to an excellent start.

But where do you go from here? The options are indeed many, far too many, in fact, for any one publication to lead you step by step toward any single given goal. But we can launch you on a process that is designed to help you find your way.

On page 74 you wrote a description of your ideal job or work situation. That's the place to start. To begin the process of reconciling your ideal with reality, the next step is to learn as much as possible about the career option you've identified. Here are some of the tools you can use:

Research

Whether that career option is a traditional one—becoming a manager in a health care organization, for example—or one that represents a more dramatic transition—opening a hunting lodge in Alaska, say—

a visit to the library and a helpful librarian or an Internet search will undoubtedly help you find at least some literature to start the quest for better understanding of what that option entails.

If you're considering a move into an already established role, you'll undoubtedly find ample resources with which to identify where and by whom that role is already being performed, as well as, in many cases, how appropriate training is acquired. That's certainly not all you'll need to know, but it's an important first step.

Even if you're considering following a road less traveled, take heart; you'll find clues to help you pick up the trail. Interested in that lodge in Alaska? Maybe the literature won't steer you directly toward that subject, but you'll certainly find leads on hunting lodges, as well as ample information on that part of the world. If your career goal is a more creative one, then it's important to be creative in your approach to better understanding it.

Reading

Consume everything you can find that discusses the option you're exploring, not only to gather more information but also to help you formulate more questions. That's what you'll need to do to get maximum mileage out of the next step.

Talk

Yes, it's now become a cliché, but remember that at the heart of every cliché lies an essential truth. In this case the essential truth is the importance of networking. Identify and talk to anyone and everyone you can find who either has had experience with the career option, might know something about it, or might know someone who does.

Once you find people whose experience parallels your goal, ask how they prepared for it, what they've learned from it, and how their expectations compared to the realities of the situation. You'll not only increase your information base; you'll begin making the contacts that may eventually help you find the right spot. You'll also begin to identify those to whom you can turn when more questions arise later on, as they inevitably will if you continue to travel toward the same goal.

What's more, the more you explore opportunities, the more likely you are to find them. Conversations often have a life of their own, and there's always the chance that in the process of talking through possibilities you'll uncover those you might not otherwise have known existed, such as the opportunity to buy into a business, join a partnership, or identify a need in the marketplace that no one else has yet filled.

Reevaluation

With every bit of information you gather, reexamine and reevaluate your goal in light of your previous perceptions and preparation for it. If what you find challenges what you thought you knew, rewrite the description of your ideal situation accordingly and see if it still fits. If not, it's time to redraft your ideal job description and begin the process again.

Time

Yes, all this will take time, and it's crucial to recognize the importance of allocating sufficient time to this important process and scheduling it into your busy life. It's essential to design specific timelines by which to systematically accomplish each step.

Of course, there is likely to be more that you will need to accomplish in managing a career change, from acquiring additional professional or managerial training to honing practical skills, such as resume writing and refining interviewing skills. Fortunately, ample resources exist to help you meet those challenges. One thing, however, should be abundantly clear: Whatever else is required to manage your career, pursuit of your goals should be a process of continual learning, analysis, reassessment, and refinement. As a trained physician, you should be well prepared to successfully meet that challenge.

Bibliography

Bolles, Richard. *The Quick Job Hunting Map.* Berkeley, Calif.: Ten Speed Press, 1975.

_____. *The Three Boxes of Life, and How to Get Out of Them.* Berkeley, Calif.: Ten Speed Press, 1978.

Butler, Timothy, and James Waldrop. *Discovering Your Career in Business.* Reading, Mass.: Addison-Wesley Publishing Company, 1996.

Byrd, Richard. *A Guide to Personal Risk Taking.* New York: AMACOM, 1974.

Cabrera, James C., and Charles F. Cabrera, Jr. *The Lifetime Career Manager.* Holbrook Mass.: Adams Media Corp., 1995.

Hagberg, Janet, and Richard Leider. *The Inventurers: Excursions in Life and Career Renewal.* Reading, Mass.: Addison-Wesley Publishing Company, 1987.

Helfand, David P. *Career Change: Everything You Need to Know to Meet New Challenges and Take Control of Your Career.* Lincolnwood, Ill.: Career Horizons, 1995.

Holland, John L. *Making Vocational Choices: A Theory of Careers.* New York: Prentice Hall, 1973.

Kimeldorf, Martin. "Job Hunting Online." *International Journal of Career Management* 7, no. 5 (1995): iii–viii.

Maitland, David. *Against the Grain.* New York: Pilgrim Press, 1981.

Pemberton, Carole, et al. "Career Orientations of Senior Executives and Their Implications for Career Guidance." *British Journal of Guidance and Counseling* 22, no. 2 (1994): 233–45.

Sheehy, Gail. *Pathfinders.* New York: William Morrow & Co., 1981.

Yeomans, William. *One Thousand Things You Never Learned in Business School: How to Get Ahead of the Pack and Stay There.* New York: McGraw-Hill, 1984.

It's your career.
If you're making a change,
we can help.

If you need concise, ready-to-use information that really addresses your unique career needs and perspectives, look to the American Medical Association (AMA) Career Management and Development books. They offer the guidance you need to make your career in medicine as satisfying and rewarding as possible.

Assessing Your Career Options, The Physician's Resume and Cover Letter Workbook, Managing the Job Interview, Evaluating and Negotiating Compensation Arrangements, Leaving the Bedside, and *Closing Your Practice* were designed to be easy to use and quick to read, with lots of helpful forms for organizing your thoughts and evaluating your professional needs. Choose the specific books you need to help polish your resume or curriculum vitae, sharpen your interviewing or negotiation skills, and chart your options for securing a successful future.

Order now.
Call the AMA at
800 621-8335.

Leaving the Bedside, Revised Edition
Order #: OP392096AIA
AMA member price: $25.95
Nonmember price: $32.95

Managing the Job Interview
Order #: OP206297AIA
AMA member price: $14.95
Nonmember price: $19.95

The Physician's Resume and Cover Letter Workbook
Order #: OP206497AIA
AMA member price: $19.95
Nonmember price: $27.95

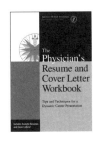

Closing Your Practice
Order #: OP381697AIA
AMA member price: $16.95
Nonmember price: $27.95

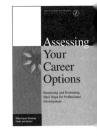

Assessing Your Career Options
Order #: OP206397AIA
AMA member price: $24.95
Nonmember price: $32.95

Evaluating and Negotiating Compensation Arrangements
Order #: OP206597AIA
AMA member price: $29.95
Nonmember price: $39.95

American Medical Association
Physicians dedicated to the health of America